A Life Well Lived
The Story of Beatrice Pearl Dickey

by Wendolyn P. Speir

Speir Publishing

A Life Well Lived
The Story of Beatrice Pearl Dickey
by Wendolyn P. Speir

ISBN-13: 978-0-9826765-9-2
Copyright © 2019 by Wendolyn P. Speir

Cover Design: Paul Michael Speir & Wendolyn P. Speir
Book Design & Production: Paul Michael Speir & Wendolyn P. Speir

Cover Background: Beatrice's favorite sweater, earrings and brooch.
Front Cover Photo: Beatrice Dickey, age 18
Back Cover Photo: Beatrice Dickey, age 88
(wearing her favorite sweater)

Manufactured in the United States

10 9 8 7 6 5 4 3 2 1

A Note Of Thanks

In the summer of 2012, I suddenly felt that I should do a book about mom's life. As the idea unfolded, it became clear that I was being called to do it, and I thank my Father God for giving me the idea.

I want to thank my mom for being so sweet and patient while I interviewed her and we went through piles and piles of pictures, and Amy for helping me find even more pictures!

I especially want to thank Mark and Paul for putting the book together and getting it published.

They made an idea become a reality.

Preface

My mom, Beatrice Pearl Dickey Wheeler Duglosch, is a very special lady! She was born in a small town in Oklahoma, the last in a family of five children.

Mom is a woman content with life no matter what comes her way. She's always been happy just making others happy! Oh, she has had heartaches and bad times, yet I have never seen a time that she didn't see the best in it, or make the best through it!! Having cancer four times and not once thinking it would get her down is one example. She always had such a positive attitude!

She loves God, and is a woman of deep faith and prayer. It's a quiet way she has of believing and living for the Lord, but that's okay! It's just her way. Some people are great preachers or wonderful, charismatic evangelists, but just as important are the sweet, smiling, gentle people who encourage others like mom does!

It has been my pleasure to care for mom, though it hasn't always been easy! We've been, quite often, like oil and water! More like gas on hot coals!! She needs to "mother" me and I need to not be, but we have found ways to get along.

If she precedes me to heaven, I have no doubt she will be sitting in a rocker on my cabin porch with a big smile, holding a steaming cup of coffee! It will be good, very good, to spend eternity with mom.

My mom. A very special lady, who will be missed tremendously when she passes from this world!

She's had a happy life for the most part, and one I think we could learn a lot from. How to love and persevere. How to accept heartache and how to forgive.

Oh, so much more could be told about Beatrice Pearl, so here is her life, as she told it to me.

May you be blessed as much as I have been!

Wendy Wheeler Speir
January, 2013

Mom said this might be Thelma, but look at those eyes! And, the ear!! My son and at least one of my grandchildren have the same ear!!!

I like to believe it is my mom!

I was born in Maysville, Oklahoma in 1925. I'm not sure, but I must have been born at home. I was the baby of five kids!

The oldest was Thelma, who we called "Sissy." Then, there was Otho Lee, who was always called "Odie." Next was Annie Pauline, Thomas Earl, and me.

–Did you live on a farm?

Yes, in the country, a ways from Paul's Valley, Oklahoma. We were very poor. Papa ran a farm and we lived in an old farmhouse with a creek running close by.

Out in the yard was an old black pot over a fire.

Papa with his mules

We had a hard life and we all had chores to do from very early on!

Mama Appie Dickey

1

–What are some of your earliest memories?

Before I started school, I had to help mama haul water up from the creek to wash clothes. I'd pour it in the black pot over and over until there was enough. Then, mama would put ashes in and let them settle down, but I'm not sure why, now. When the wash water was just right, we'd wash and wash the clothes. It was hard work!!

* * *

One time, oh I was about six or seven, Earl and I would climb up on top of the barn. Well, we did it a lot, but one time I got hurt!

That roof was made of tin pieces that over lapped each other. I slipped and ran my hand under one of the pieces of tin and cut it open badly! (Chuckling to herself) Ooohhh...That's not a good memory!

* * *

Don't remember much before age five, except for one Christmas. Mama would put up socks and papa would come along and put oranges, apples and nuts in each one. That's all we could afford, but it was really a treat for us!!

Papa

Thelma and Odie

The only other memory I have was way back at age two or three and it was of something papa did for me.

He had walked all the way off to Paul's Valley one time. I waited for him all day by the window and finally I saw him walking along towards the house. On his shoulders he had a little rocking chair for me!!

* * *

Oh! I remember another chore I had to do! Mama and I would carry lunch to papa and Odie, who were farming across the creek.

Mama would fix the food and put it all in a big metal washtub. We'd carry it down to our side of the creek. She had tied a rope to one handle so she could toss it across for papa to catch. Then, he pulled the tub across the creek, so they could eat and rest awhile.

* * *

Farming was the way we lived. I remember papa, well, Thelma, Pauline and Odie, too, would all go out to pick cotton. Earl was only about ten at the time.

I guess I was about six or seven—old enough to want to go help, too! I begged mama to make me a cotton sack, so I could go help them!

4

Odie

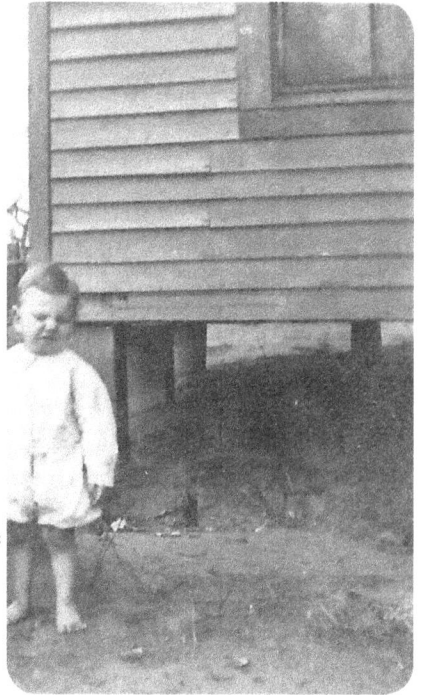

Most of our pictures were burned up in the fire.

Thelma and Odie

5

–Did you ever go to church or other places as a family?

Hmmm...I don't think so. Well, I'm sure we did, 'cause I remember Odie and Sissy were baptized in the river by Maysville. Of course, I just remember them telling about it!

Our closest neighbor was a little old lady—don't remember her name. She invited us all down to dinner one time. She had caught a big turtle and cooked it outside in a big pot.

When she cut it, there were seven layers of meat in different colors! I don't know what else she cooked, but I remember it was sooooooo good!

That's about the only time I remember going anywhere with the whole family.

The trip from Oklahoma to Texas.

We lived in Maysville until I was nearly eight, then we moved to Texas.

On the trip, I rode in the cab of the truck with mama and the driver we hired. Earl and Pauline rode in the back with all our stuff. Once in awhile, I would crawl through the window in the back of the truck to go sit with them.

Papa, Sissy, and Odie had gone on to Texas ahead of time because she was real sick with sinus problems. We came on in a truck through San Antonio and drove on down to Stockdale. We settled in Pandora.

I remember going to Seals Chapel school, which was my first school in Texas.

Before school—I don't know how long after we got there—I got real sick and had to have my tonsils taken out. Uncle Dick took me and mama to Nixon to Dr. Elder's to have the surgery. Ooooh, they were so infected and I was so little and sick!

Afterward, we went to Uncle Dick's house. I remember some things about that time.

The next morning, he put me on his knee and fed me soft corn flakes out of a goblet glass.

Isn't it something how I remember all those things?!

After surgery, I had boils real bad on my legs and had one on my face that had to be lanced. Mama and Odie took care of me. We were at the Fridge place then.

* * *

Oh. I remember one other thing that happened at school. I had gotten a pretty China Doll from someone and had taken it to school one day.

It was an old wooden school house with steps that were open underneath. I was playing with my doll on those steps when a boy ran into me. I fell under the steps and my doll's head got broken. Oh I was just heartbroken! We didn't get too many toys back then!

8

Appie, Aunt Osie, Aunt Pearl, Aunt Ann and Aunt Jessie

Aunt Pearl's house on Kayton Ave.

–*Mom! I just had a thought, how you always wanted us to have a small rocker or a pretty doll! It must have been because of those memories of things you loved!*

Yes, I'm sure that's why!

–*What else do you remember from your childhood? You visited Aunt Pearl in San Antonio, 'cause I've heard you tell about the house on Kayton.*

One time, Uncle Tom, Aunt Pearl's husband, brought a watermelon home. We went outside to cut it up and eat it. Man! I thought that was so much fun, but then, I was just a kid.

Shy Bea (age 17) with Sylvia and Wanda

About that time, Sissy had to have surgery, so we moved again. Mama came to San Antonio with her, but we all stayed out in the country with papa.

It was up to me to cook breakfast for everyone! I was only about eleven then!!

Papa would go milk early in the morning and bring some milk in to the kitchen. He'd put a pan of it on the back of the stove to warm, so I could get busy making biscuits. We all had to do chores to help out!

–*What kind of work did Grandpa do?*

Well, back then he and Odie worked on the WPA, working on the roads for the county. We moved so many places, so I don't know where we went next. They would always farm wherever we lived.

We always had a cow and mules to pull the plow and wagon.

Appie Dickey, Thelma, Earl, Pauline, Mamie Bell,
Minnie, Odie, Claude Rhodes, Herbert, Bea (18), Wanda.

Minnie

Odie

In all these years up to when I was about fifteen, we moved so much, but ended up in Verdi, near Leming. We had a little old country house, but mama fixed it up real nice. From there, we moved to San Antonio.

By then, Odie and Minnie had married, so he didn't go with the family. I didn't want to leave school in Pleasanton, so I stayed with Mary Suggs to finish out the school year.

When school was out, I came on up to San Antonio. I was sixteen by then and we lived on Buena Vista street.

2506 Buena Vista. Huh! How did I remember that?!

Beatrice Pearl, age 16

Fox Tech graduating class of '45. Beatrice Dickey, age 19. (2nd row, 1st from left).

Earl Dickey, 3rd from left.

I started Tech High and graduated there in 1945.

–What did grandpa do for work in San Antonio?

Oh. He was the night watchman at the Milam Building downtown.

Earl was a fireman and drove a cab.

–What did grandma do?

She kept house and always worked in the fields with papa before we moved up to San Antonio, but she never worked outside the home.

Lowell Irvin Dickey

I was about 17. I thought this red suit was so pretty!

–Well, what did you do while in high school?

Oh my goodness, honey! The first summer I worked at Walgreen's downtown on the fountain side. The next summer, I worked on the medicine side. Before my senior year, I worked at Woolworth's across the street from Walgreen's on Houston Street.

–What type of job did you do?

I was just a clerk, waiting on people and I'd put merchandise out. I didn't work there long.

After I graduated, I went to live with Odie and Minnie and got a job at a beauty shop in Pleasanton. Oh my! Hamilton was the name of the owner! My friend, Henrietta also worked there. She had a little black dog that she couldn't keep.

I took the dog and named him Rags. When I got married, I gave him to Sissy and mama, because we moved to an apartment that didn't allow pets.

Bea Dickey, ages 16-19

Pretty Lady!
Age 19

Graduation Day

This was a butter yellow dress I wore to graduation.

Going to work in Pleas-
anton, I got a ride with E.J.
Collins. I didn't work there very
long, because I got very sick
with an ear infection.

Before long, I moved back
to San Antonio, and got a job
at Kelly's Beauty Shop out on
Blanco Road.

That's when I met your dad.

Odie with Rags.

This is what Wendell looked like
when I met him, even though it's a
few years later.

Papa and me. I was 19 here.

When I was working at Kelly's, someone from work asked me to go to Marble Falls with a few other people.

I sure wanted to go, but knew mama would throw a fit! But, Aunt Ann said, "Now Appie, there's not one thing wrong with her going! They're just going to fish and have fun!!"

Aunt Jessie, Mama, Aunt Ann, Aunt Ora (Papa's sister), Aunt Pearl, Aunt Bea (Papa's sister).

So, I got to go, thanks to Aunt Ann! I was about 21 at the time.

Earl and I (about age 21) at a family get together.

–So, tell me, how did you meet dad?

Oh well, Smitty and Esther—you know, Uncle Lee's brother—knew him. Wendell worked downtown doing car upholstery and he met Smitty.

They told him about me and me about him. We finally met and got to talking on the phone.

That was around November and at Christmas, he came to the house for dinner and to meet everyone.

He went with mama to go get the turkey—can you imagine?! He helped with cooking the dinner and even cleaned the house some! He was so friendly!!

One thing I remember the most about that time is when he took me to the Majestic Theater. Of course, I had never been before, or done anything like it!

The theater was so pretty! When you looked up, it was like staring up at a night sky with stars everywhere.

–How old were you?

I was 25! We got married the following February!

Bea (age 17) with cousin Norman.

Oh! But, on New Year's Eve, Smitty and Esther wanted us to go to Helotes to a dance.

(Laughing)

I had just bought a pair of brown suede high heel shoes. Oh how I thought I was really dressed up that night!

Afterward, we were to spend the night at Smitty and Esther's.

I had never done anything like that, but they were so nice to us!

I remember Esther making breakfast for us with the best biscuits!

The night before, Wendell had asked me to marry him and gave me a ring. He took me home right after breakfast.

I just think back on all the things I didn't know or didn't do then. I was so immature!

Mama didn't let me do anything or go anywhere.

Young Bea about 17

27

–Where did you marry?

At home, 2506 Buena Vista, in mama's house. In her living room.
Aunt Pearl came over to sing for us. It was just a simple ceremo-
ny.

My friend that I worked with, Sharon and her daughter, Patsy
came. Let's see. Ella and Norman Leo, Lavina, Elise and, of course,
Grandma Dunn were there. Odie and Minnie, Earl and Belle and
Pauline, but Lee was working.

Ruby Jean, Norman Leo, Janice, Bea, (Sharon), Jo, and Elise.

Bea, Jo and Ruby Jean were there, too. I think Janice and Robert Earl were about nine and ten at the time.

Wedding shower at Minnie
and Odie's.

Wendell with his new mother in law and his mom.

31

Odie, Lavina, Esther, Smitty, Robert Earl and Janice.

Jo, Bea and Lillian Beatrice.

You know, I never thought to wear a white dress! All I wanted was a nice blue dress! Isn't that something?

I remember that the candles wouldn't stand up straight, so Minnie and Odie would go by and fix them over and over.

(Chuckles)

Funny the little things you remember!

Grandma Dunn, Lavina, and Elise.

Right before we were married, we went up to Fort Worth so I could meet them. I sure thought I was something else to be going away from San Antonio alone with Wendell.

I'll never forget how Earl went back to my bedroom after the wedding. He gave me a big hug and a wedding card. We were always very close!

Back before I married, I'd go to visit Earl and Belle and stay overnight. Earl would be working, so Belle and I would just talk and talk.

And, one time, Reg and Earline and Ella and Slim took me down to Padre Island. I was about 25. I remember sleeping in the back of the car and the water would hit near the car all night! Oh, I just knew that car was going in the ocean!!

You can see the car and the water in the back here. That's one of Reg and Earline's children on the table.

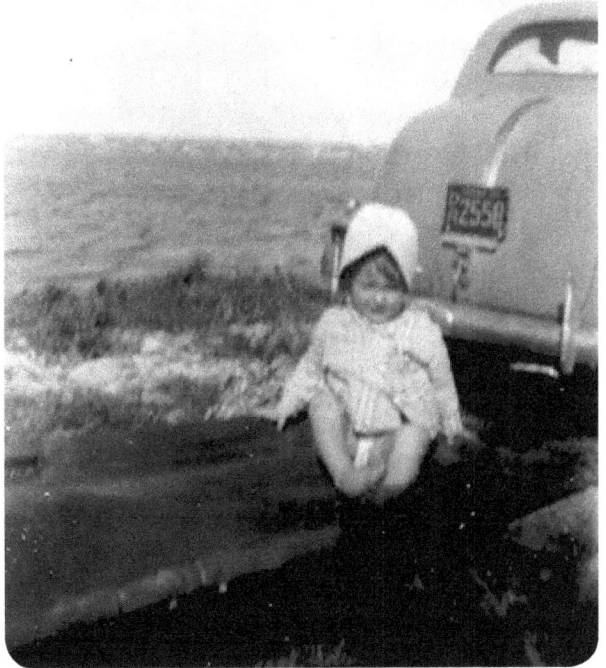

Oh! I also would ride the Greyhound bus down to Minnie and Odie's. The bus went right into Leming and let me off in front of their store. Then, on Sunday, they'd take me home.

−Do you remember the lady in front of the store?

Oh yes! (Smiling big) She was a little Mexican lady that lived nearby. She could make the best tortillas!!

Once in awhile she would stop by the store and stand outside to talk to us. She never would come inside, though.

Such a nice lady!!

While I was there with Odie and Minnie, I went to a Bar-B-Q at the Catholic Church. I went with Bernice--remember, the post office mistress?

−Yes! She was always so nice to me! Man! She must have worked there a long time!

She was a good friend and we went to the Bar-B-Q, even though it was sooooo cold!

–I loved Aunt Sissy's house!! Remember the good dinners she fixed and put on the big table? I loved the big porch! I'd run out one door, around and in the other door, And the claw foot tub! It was always an adventure going there!!

When I got back to the house, Minnie warmed bricks and put them in towels in the bed. Oh how warm the bed was and it felt so good to my feet!

This was probably right after I graduated.

In San Antonio, when I'd go to work, I had to ride the bus, after walking a long way. I was so scared!

One time, someone followed me, which really scared me! After that, Herbert, Sissy's husband, would meet me and walk me home from the bus stop.

–Mom, I love this picture of Aunt Sissy! This is how I remember her! She was such a sweet lady & showed me so much love! Well, I bet she was that way to everyone!!

–Well, let's get back to your wedding. What was it like?

We weren't going to church anywhere and just wanted to have a small wedding.

–Where was grandpa? You said you were married at grandma's house.

Well, he just didn't come. I think they were separated at the time. We had a buffet table and a table spread with a cake and punch. That's where the candles that wouldn't stand up straight were.

A Methodist pastor from down the street came to marry us. When everyone left, and we did, too, Wendell drove around and around, 'cause he just knew Smitty and Esther were following us!

(Laughing)

Right after we married, we lived on Ave. B and Wendell worked for a car dealership.

We didn't live there long, because he went to Bryan to teach how to do car upholstery. I was working, so I stayed with mama.

–You didn't want to go with him?

No. He went up there first and bought a small trailer. He fixed it up real nice for me. I joined him after awhile.

Before long, we came back with the trailer and parked it outside mama and Sissy's house. They had never seen anything like it before!

We moved it to some trailer park and that's when I had Linda.

One time, Wendell got the mumps, so we went over to live with mama and Sissy. We stayed there until he got better and could go back to work. It wasn't too long after this that we moved to California.

–Did you take the trailer?

No. It was just a small mobile home and he sold it.

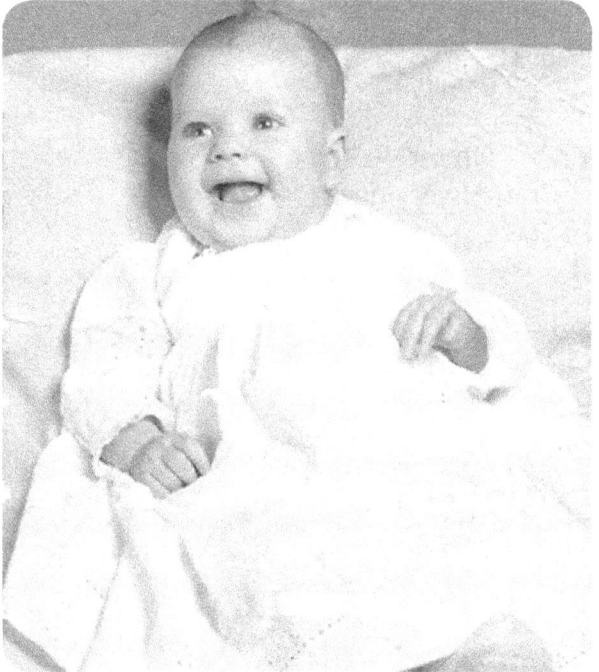

I'll never forget when we moved to California. We left here pulling a car called a Nash. The seats folded down so we could sleep in it. We went through Colorado, but all I remember is that the car started going really slow. We stopped to check it out and when we stepped out we stepped into a lot of snow! When we left Texas it was 100°!! Where we stopped a man told us nothing was wrong with the car, it was just going uphill and working harder!

First, we went to Portland, Oregon, and Oh! It rained all the time!! Linda was in diapers and we had to wash and hang them in a basement! I told Wendell one day that I couldn't stand it, so he said we'd just move on to California.

Oh my! It rained every day. Every day!

So, we loaded up and moved down. We first went to Sacramento, I think. That's where we met Rosie and Jean. He worked in the Folsom Prison as a guard. We just spent the night with them.

–What?! You didn't even know them and just spent the night?

No, well, I don't really remember that time too much.

Linda - The linoleum
I talk about.

We had these plastic drapes for a long time!

Linda, age 5 and Wendy, age 2.

From there, we went on to El Cerrito and rented a little house, like in a housing area. It wasn't very nice, with wooden floors and just one wooden table.

Wendell got everything in and said it would be just fine when I got the tablecloth on and the beds made.

Linda was nine months old then. The first thing he did was put pretty linoleum down on the floors. I had plastic drapes I put up.

Man! That was 60 years ago!!

One day, here comes Wendell with a rocking chair for me!

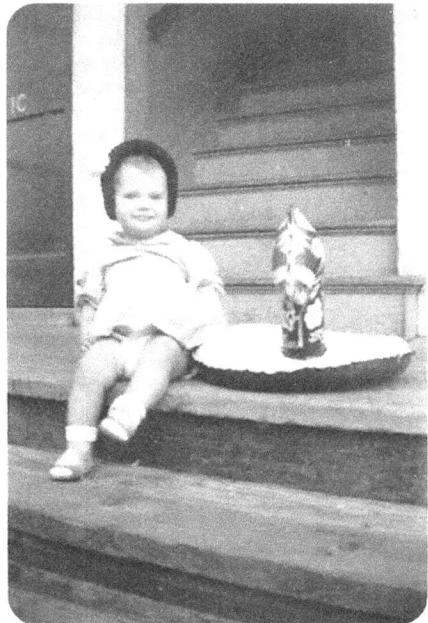

—You know mom, that's why you always want a rocking chair! A good memory!

I remember, too, that New Year's Eve we went to a dance.

    It was at a ballroom. I had never been to anything like it!
The room was so big and the floor was so shiny. I really don't remember much except it was so much fun! And, the orchid!!! I was so
surprised when Wendell brought me the beautiful gold orchid!

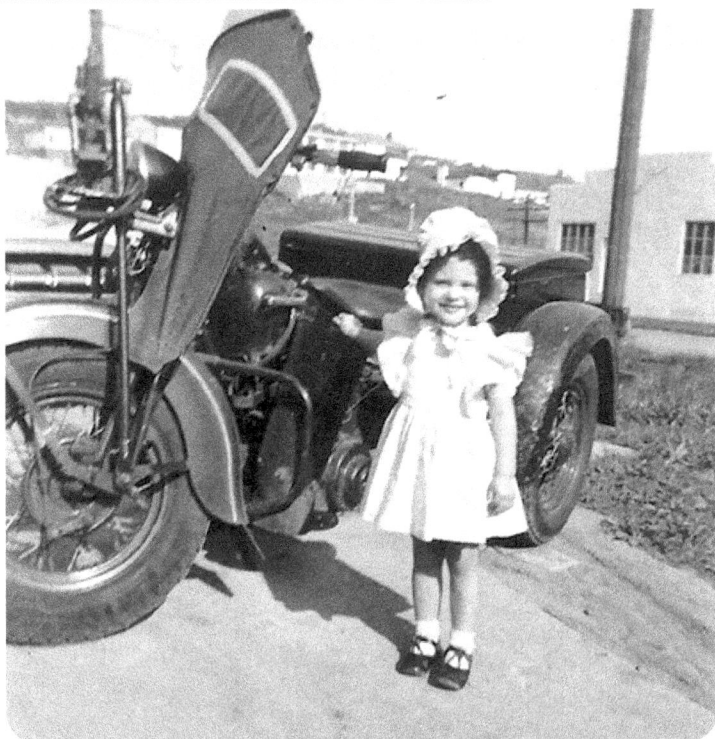

Linda wearing a bonnet Grandma Dickey made for her.

After the time in the little house, we moved above the upholstery shop. That's where we met Johnny and Louise.

He worked with Wendell in the shop.

I remember she couldn't speak much English - I think they were French.

I remember one time I had to go downtown in Wendell's car with a stick shift. I asked Louise to go with me. (Chuckling) I must have stalled out the car on too many times, 'cause when we got back she said, "I no go with you any more!"

We lived there a long time, because you were born there.

Christmas '55

Proud Grandma!

–She is smiling 'cause she pinched me and made me cry! Ha Ha!

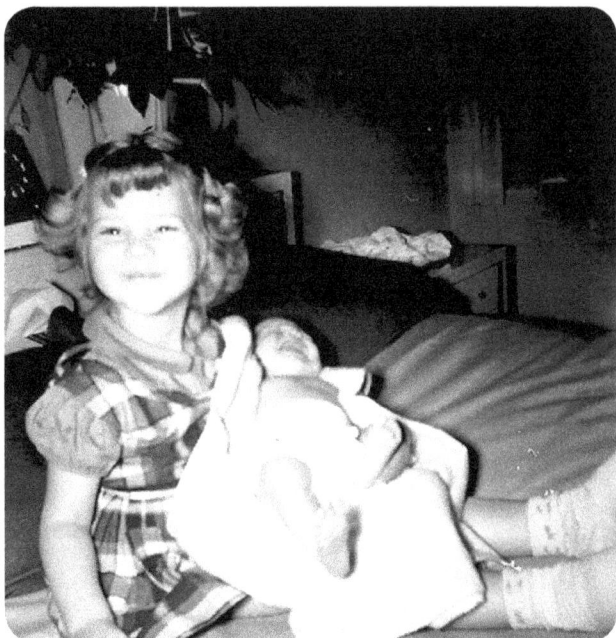

Linda, age 3 and Wendy, 2 days old.

49

Mama came out to stay with Linda while I went to have you. She was going to stay a couple of months, but got so homesick. Wendell told her that it'd be okay for her to go back; that we'd do okay. She had never been away from home before!

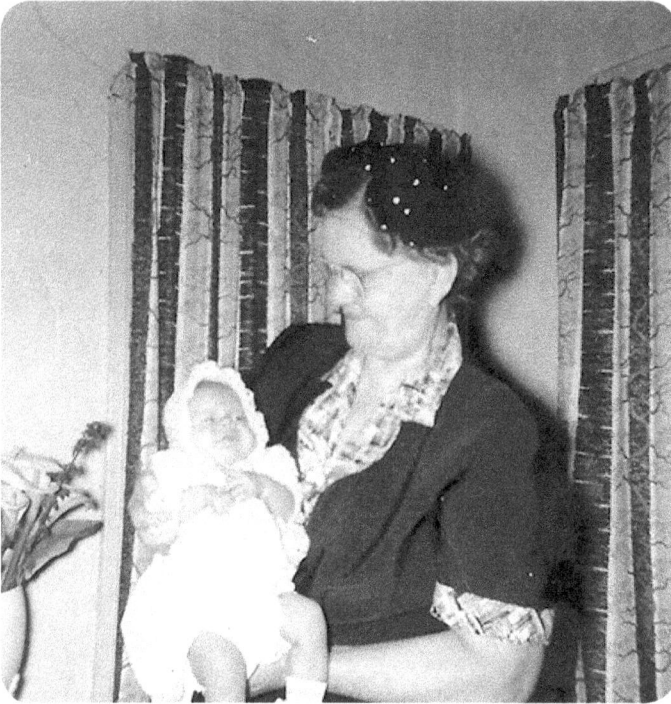

I think she stayed two weeks. Oh! Just had another memory! When mama got to our house, she had two venison steaks in her suitcase! Earl had sent them to me! They were still frozen, too!

We lived up above the shop until you were three, then we moved to San Pablo, across the street from Ray and Laura.

–*Well, mom, I have a lot of good memories from that time, yet I was so little!*

50

*–Easter was always dress up time!!
And you always made a really cool
bunny cake!*

Looks like someone ate on his eyes!

–I have good memories of playing outside with Linda.

–You always dressed us up so cute!

Yes. Mama made a lot of dresses and bonnets. Oh! And bloomers! (Laughing)

Linda always loved dogs.

Wendy, age 3.

Pretty lady!

—Dad was always building something and cooking outside! I remember that chaise lounger in this picture. It was such an amazement to me that he could build it! I loved going out to lay on it. Those are such good memories!

We lived up on a hill and the elementary school was down the hill and across a field. That's where Linda started school.

We had a lot of fun with Laura and Ray!! We had dinners and went camping, but the first time we went anywhere with them was to Lake Tahoe.

We rented a cabin up on a hill and oh! How much snow there was! The cabin had one level with a sleeping loft. The ladder to it went straight up!

You, Linda, Sherrie and Dickie slept up there.

–I remember that!! It was sooooo scary up there! I remember the large wooden walls and the smell of fresh cut lumber.
   We had so much fun going down the hill on toboggans!

Yes, and you were only a little over three at the time!

We were really good friends with Ray and Laura. We went to the lake and rivers to camp and boat quite often and for several years.

We went other places, like Disneyland, too. We just always had so much fun together!!

Those were good times and good memories!

I was scared silly of the water!!

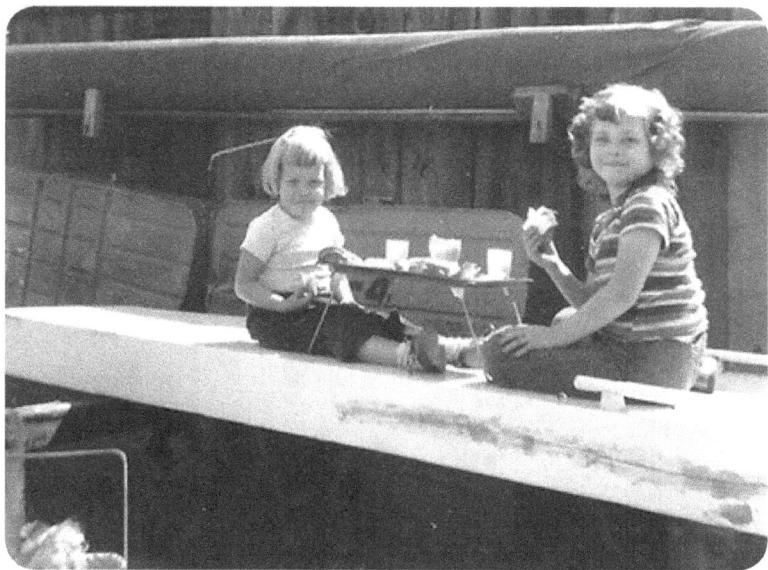

We had so much fun!

–Mom, I have good memories of dad building a boat.

Yes, it was when you were three to about five and Linda was six to nine. We went down to where Wendell was building it and you girls would play on it.

I'd fix you lunches and you always enjoyed yourselves so much! We even had Easter there one year!

One time, Grandma Dunn and Winnie and Vee came to visit. They couldn't believe he could do such a thing!!

We took it out on the ocean when it was done and one time the waves got so huge we had to go back to shore.

My favorite picture of dad.

Dad loved the water, being on a boat and fishing.

Lilian Beatrice

Wendell would go deep sea diving and go fishing–always catching HUGE fish. We often had company that loved to go out on the boat.

I remember one time that Lillian Beatrice and a friend came out to visit.

My goodness! That's been a long time ago!!

We also went to the lake and on picnics a lot. It was great fun camping-most of the time at Lake Berryessa in Napa Valley.

–I can still see you & dad fixing up the camp!! He would hang big tarps from tree to tree to make an enclosure, then he'd dig a deep hole and put a "toilet" over it that he had made from a camp stool. We put up tents and have a kitchen area. Man did the bacon ever smell good cooking out in the open!

Mom always made life fun for us!!!!

–Mom, do you remember when dad took me sailing in San Francisco Bay? I was around 11 or 12 and it was so cool going under the Golden Gate Bridge!! It was fantastic and so much fun!!!

Yes, boating was some of our best times!!!

–Mom, I remember a little lady we went to see.

Oh, well that was Grandma Messick, who we called Cripple Grandma.

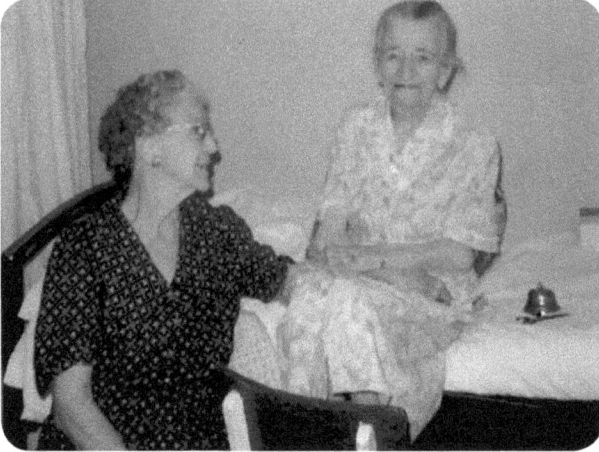

–Some of my best memories were in San Francisco!

Yes, we would go to eat and to Chinatown, or to Fisherman's Wharf. We went down the most curving road and saw movies at a huge cinema. Oh! The sourdough bread was so good from the Wharf!

We'd get some cheese and drive to the beach to watch the boats while we ate.

Wendell and Bea and Paul Tillis.

Bea, pregnant with Wendy.

Jonna Tillis

Another place we always enjoyed going was to Sacramento to cousins Johnny Ruth and Paul.

We went for Thanksgiving just before I had you. Linda and Jonna had fun playing and we all cooked the dinner.

When you were three we went back for a visit. You and Linda rode on their horse.

—That's one of my best memories! I can still think of all the fun we had going out in the

tomato fields or to the homes of the Filipino workers. And, I can imagine you don't know what all we did in the barn! You would have had a fit to know we climbed so high on the HUGE tractors. It was so much fun!

Linda, Odie and Bea.

Appie, Minnie, Bea, Odie, Herbert, and Thelma.

In the summer of '58 we came back to Texas to visit everyone. Being at Odie and Minnie's store was a great adventure!

Lee, Pauline and Janice came to visit us. Sam, Nell and kids came, too. Mama came up from her house, and Sissy came, too. We had a great time of visiting!

Odie would take you and Linda out to see his dogs and you really enjoyed that!

–Yes! I remember Aunt Minnie letting me get candy and little toys out of big jars in the store. Oh how good the Vanilla Wafers were!

Pauline, Bea, Janice, and Appie at Minnie and Odie's store.

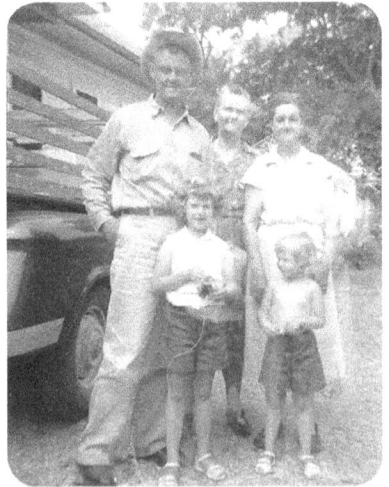

Linda and Wendy with Uncle Odie, Grandma, and Aunt Sissy.

You girls loved dogs, turtles, bunnies–well, any animals! We always had a dog or two while you were growing up.

That's my red Pekingese, Sweety Pie, that Wendell gave me.

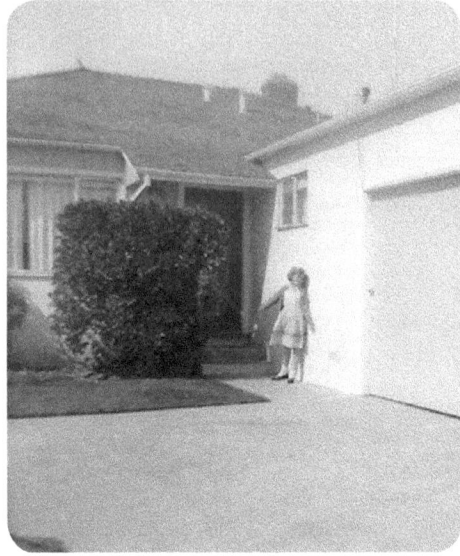

—Mom, I remember that we lived in many different houses and that you always fixed each one up so pretty! Every Christmas you decorated the house up special-made the holiday so much fun for us! I seem to remember the holidays the most, but I have good memories of each house. Moving so many times was very hard on us all, but you did your best to remain calm and make the best of it for us.

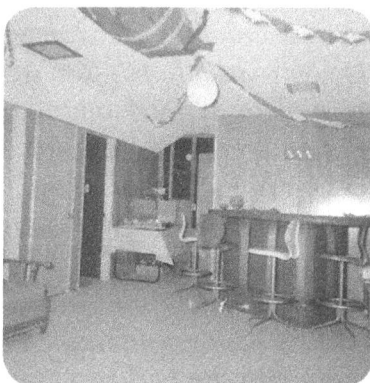

We moved to Fremont when you were eight and Linda was eleven. The housing development was brand new and we had to put in all the yard in front and back.

–Yes, I remember finding some tiny pink mice out back and brought them in to show you. You weren't happy at all! Haha

The house was a two story with a basement as the bottom floor. Wendell put in a bathroom and bedroom and finished it all off so nice We had several parties there.

–I use to sneak into the stairwell and watch you! I remember the meals you made there. You were the best cook!!!
There were many good memories in Fremont. We went camping quite often and many people came to visit. I remember Thanksgiving Day being a special time. You could cook the best turkey and dressing!! And here we are, 50 years later, still having dinner around the same table!!
There were bad times as well, but through it all mom did her best to make us happy, and make life good. She taught me how to take the good with the bad and make the best of it.

–I really wasn't drinking!

At mom's 80th birthday.

We went to visit papa
and Agnes before he died.

*–I remember going to see
them and how sweet they
both were to me.*

We came by train to San Antonio to visit everyone when you were seven, nine, and right before you were 13, we moved back. One time, we all went to Brown's Mexican Restaurant and had a party. We had a blast and lots of good food!

We'd go down to Minnie and Odie's and visit with Lee and Pauline. Minnie would take us shopping in San Antonio, which was always a great time!!

Minnie and Odie's house was always "the place" to meet and mama lived with them for awhile. Of course, Minnie kept us all laughing with funny stories and sayings!

And, oh could she cook! There was always a feast at Minnie and Odie's house!

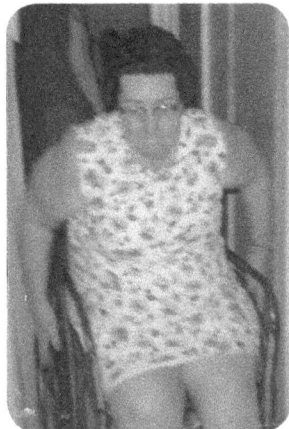

—Mom, I can't believe that we kept these all these years!

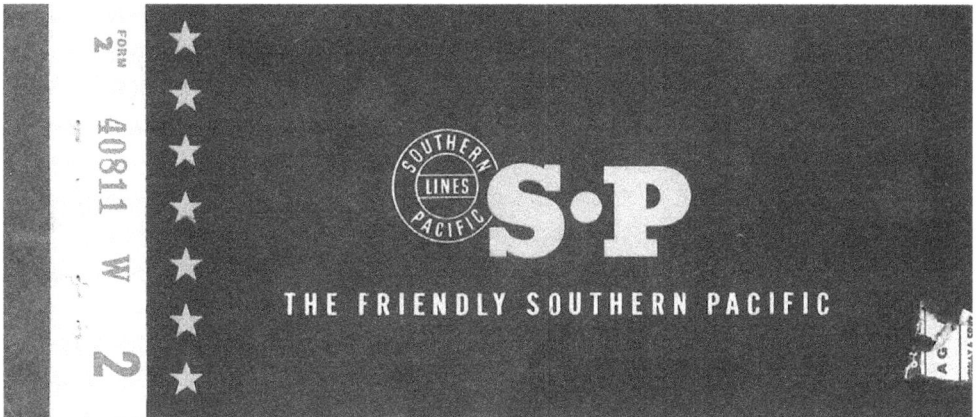

Train tickets from Oakland, CA to San Antonio, TX in 1962.
It cost $9.35, one way, for the three of us!

Mr. and Mrs. Carpenter. The best bosses ever!

R&E Cleaners on Clark.

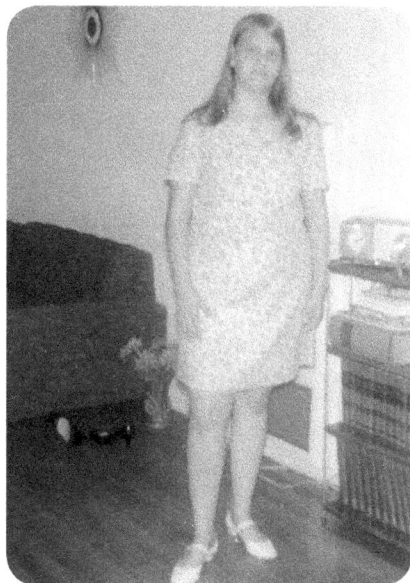

The living room on Lyric. Wendy,
age 13.

In December of 1967 we moved back to San Antonio for good. It was a sad time, but we had family around ready to help us. Earl helped me find a car and the house on Lyric Street.

I got a job at R & E cleaners and had wonderful employers! Mr and Mrs carpenter became good friends and even gave you your first job!

–Yes, she was a great lady! What good memories!!

At this time Linda and Ray married and we had the reception at the house. She was a beautiful bride!

We lived there for awhile, then Lee found a house down the street from them on McDougal.

It was in this house that you started high school and I started working at J. C. Penny.

–I remember how much we liked the house and we had good memories there! Our sweet Nicoe was fun to have around and it was there that you met Bob.

One of my favorite memories was the Christmas there that you gave me my Mother's ring. I was so happy!

The Story of Beatrice Pearl Dickey

Working at J.C. Penny's.

Our sweet Nicoe.

—Mom, I was so proud of you when you went to get the job at Penney's! It was probably the hardest thing you've ever done, but you did it!

You learned things you had never done and you did them well! Everyone loved "Duggie"!!!

You were a great employee and the retirement party they held for you showed that love!

Retirement party at JC Penny's, 1990.

During this time, we went up to Earl and Belle's cabin at Medina Lake quite often. It was "the" place to go and the family got together as often as they could.

We always had good times and lots of good food! Earl and Odie would go fishing and bring in HUGE catfish, then we'd have a fish fry and stuff ourselves! It was great fun!

–I loved going swimming off the dock, but was always a bit scared of the fish I knew had to be right there! It was so neat to go with Uncle Earl when he ran his lines and see him pull up the huge catfish.

I was so glad Minnie got to go that time! She didn't get to go many places and really had a great time!!!

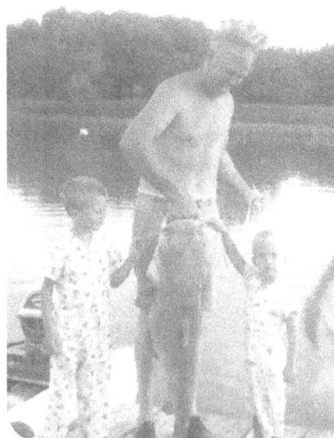

—Mom, wasn't the reunion time a lot of fun, too? I can still see Aunt Minnie hurrying around and everyone setting up camp. She'd give orders and no one thought to disagree! She knew what to do for sure!!!

One year, she had a "theme" for the girls and women which brought lots of laughter. We all made and wore long culottes.

—It seems silly now, but it was a style back then.

Three generations of Beatrice's.

There was always loads of good food! Everyone enjoyed talking, playing games and taking lots of pictures.

—When we had it up on the hill in Austin, it was so beautiful looking out over the land and river. We could see the capital building, too. A few of us kids would climb down and go to the water, but we just walked through the forest and swung on large vines.

When we lived on McDougal, I met Bob Duglosch.

He loved going to the lake and fishing with Earl! He just fit right in with the family!!

One day, we were eating lunch when Earl called. He said the fish were HUGE and wanted us to come up. So, we hurried around and got things together and were on our way up to the lake in no time! Bob loved it so much!!!

Marriage of Robert Duglosch
and Beatrice Wheeler
July 1, 1972

On our honeymoon in California.

–Yes! You took me on the trip, too, which was very strange!

We had to take his grand daughter home and we stopped to visit his family along the way.

When we got to California, we found out that Linda was very ill and in a hospital in San Francisco. What a trip that was!

We went to Fremont to visit with Ray's parents, as that was where Ray was, who was three at the time.

Fremont, CA.

In 1972 we moved out to the country and took care of two horses for the property owner. It was great for a short time.

Bob and I opened a small restaurant with his sister, Bea. She and I got to be good friends.

It all came to a quick end when Bob had a heart attack and died.

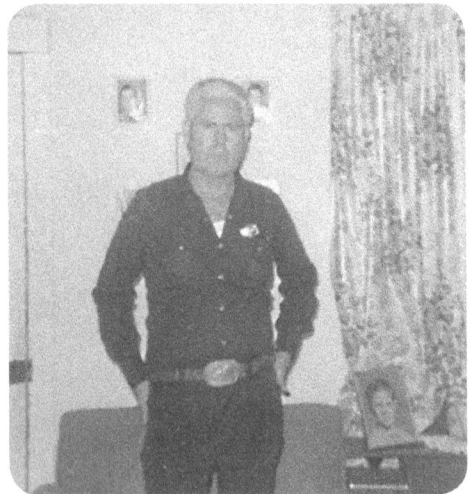

Odie and Earl helped me find a mobile home and we moved back into town when Bob passed away. You were in high school still.

I loved my little house!

Always on the phone!

You loved to cook in your kitchen.

It snowed in 1973.

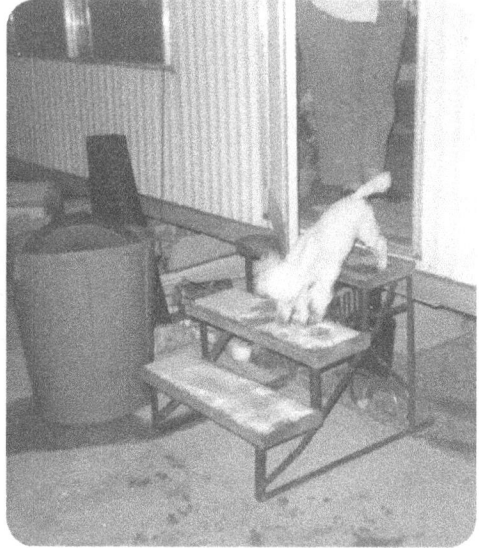

We couldn't drive very well in it, and Nicoe sure did not want to go out to potty!

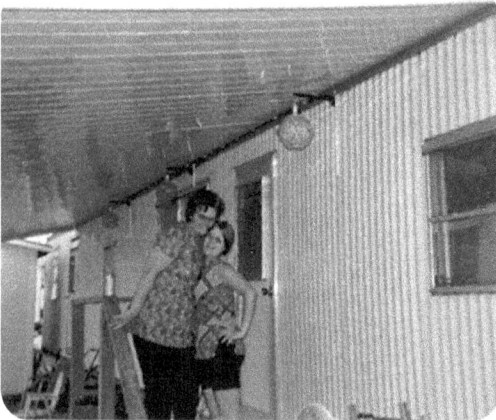

Ray, Linda and Raymie came for a visit on their way through Texas.

You graduated in May of '73 and dated Mike until you married a year later.

We had a lot of fun that year getting ready for the wedding.

Aunt Minnie and you made your dress. You were so beautiful!

During the 70 and 80's, you and the kids lived with me off and on. It made me so happy! I loved having the grand kids around.

Uvonne and I loved baby Mark!

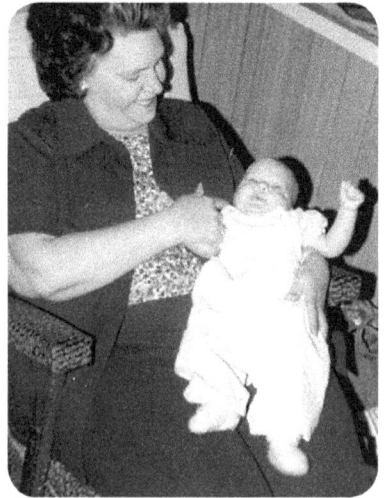

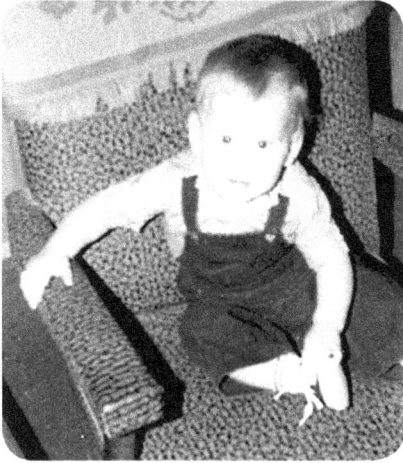

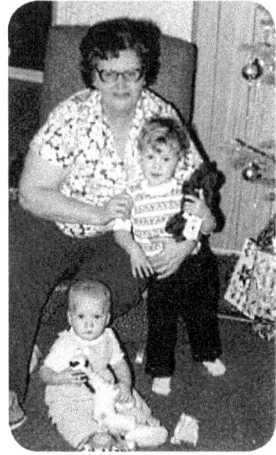

Grandma Bea with Mark & Amy.

The mobile home wasn't very big, but we moved things around and made room. There was no way I'd have you anywhere else while Mike was overseas. I loved the babies, then little ones playing, laughing and having fun!

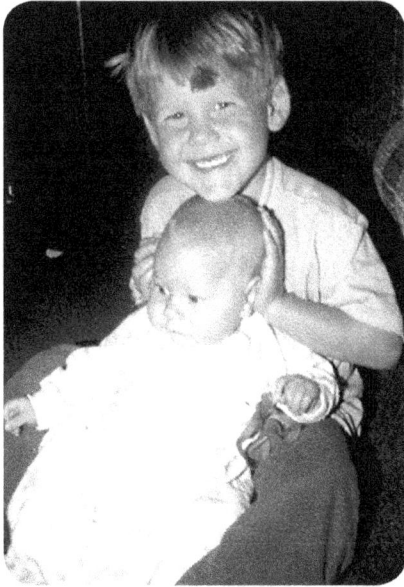

—You always enjoyed your home and welcomed anyone who came over. It was a home filled with love, happiness and always good food!

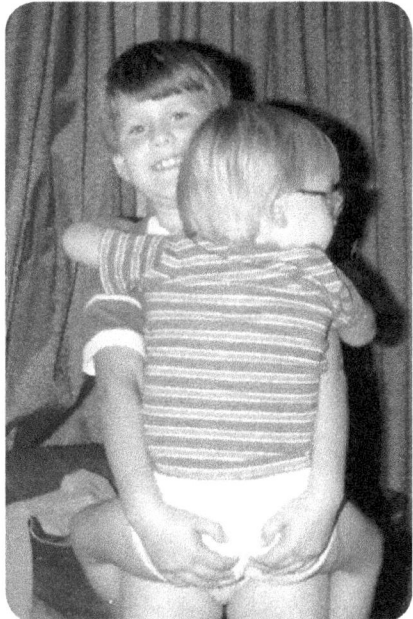

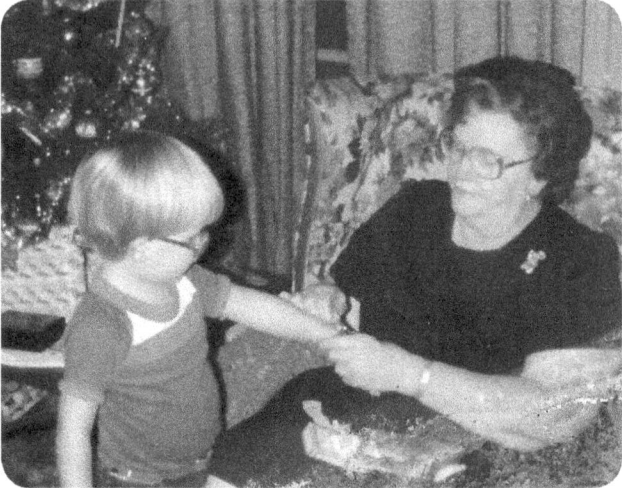

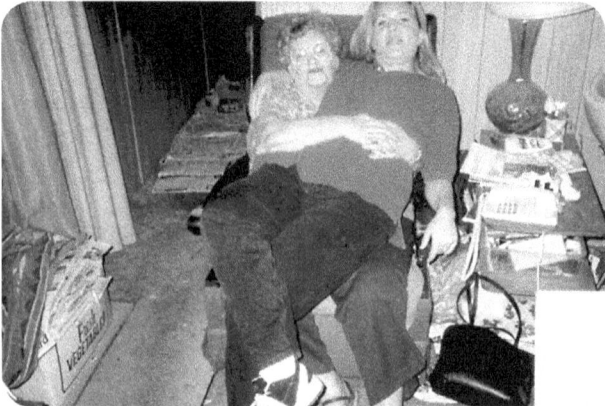

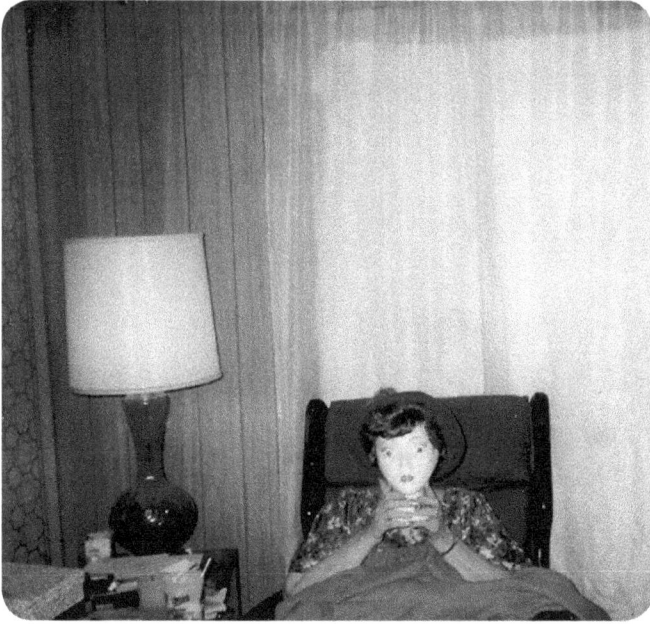

You hated the wig and didn't want me taking pictures of you.

–We had to move when you had cancer. The mobile home was so old and the floors were no longer safe. You needed to not do stairs. You always kept a good outlook and never gave up or thought you'd die! Your faith in God's love and your loving spirit saw you through!

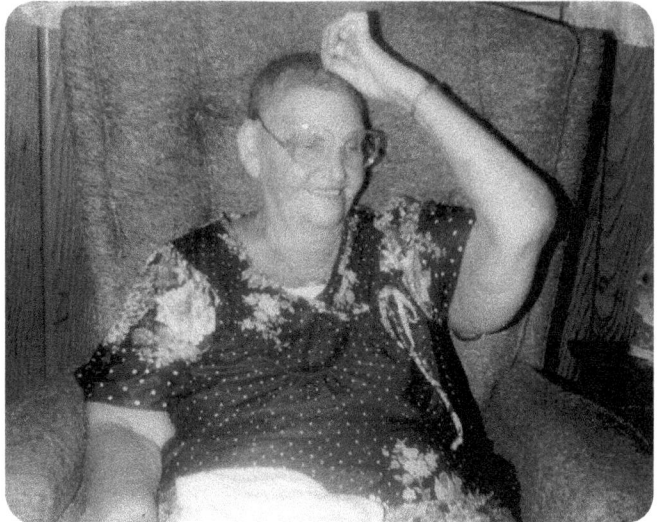

We moved to an apartment while I was getting over surgery and I was able to go back to church. It didn't take long before we knew we needed a house. You and Paul went to see about one and we took it right away! We were going to fix it up and you did some painting, but there was always something to keep us from doing more.

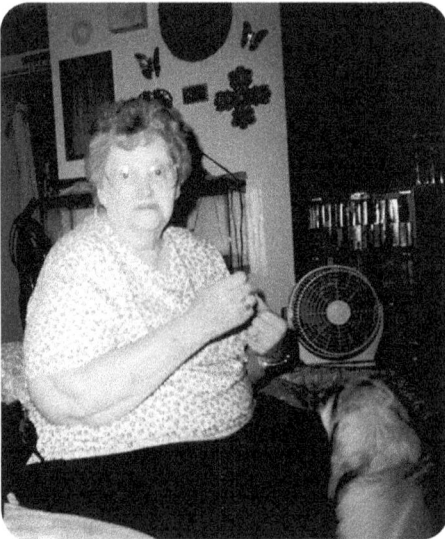

—Mom. We sure loved the house on Hicks! It quickly became one with an open door, but it was good to help so many people!!

Yes! A lot of people came to stay awhile, then move on. Some came back more than once! (Laughing) One night Kevin and Kathy came to the door looking for Bryan. They had no place to live, so we took them in!

—Well, it wasn't hard to do! Paul & Bryan had already turned the garage into a room, so Kevin went there and Kathy took my room! We gave our rooms up a lot, didn't we mom?!

We sure did, but that was good to do!!! Let's see, Paul came more than once and with Stacy and Tristan for awhile. Before that, Gilby and Amy and kids came up from Poteet to stay awhile, then Mike came and stayed three years!

—We loved helping all the ones who came our way, and it was not only a big house, it was a house full of God's love!

In 2002 I got real sick with my blood sugar, which put me in the hospital, then a nursing home.

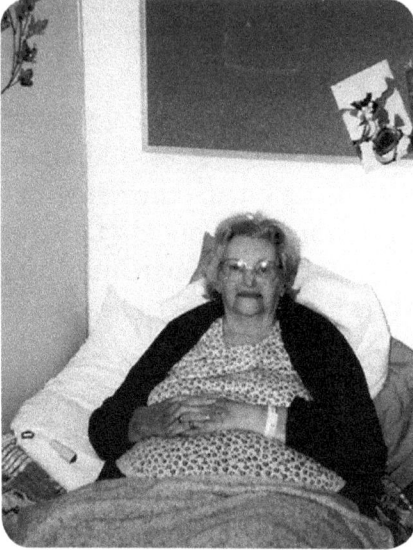

−Yes, you nearly died! Oh how sick you were!! But, you still had a happy spirit and found things to pass the time. You loved sitting outside talking with people and watching them come and go, and you enjoyed talking to the nurses. It wasn't long, though, until you were ready to go home!!!

—I found out I could take you home on a program that was like having you in a nursing home, so we moved back to San Antonio.

It was good to be home!! Before long, Janice and Bob came to visit. Mike came to live with us, and Amy and her family, too!

(Laughing) We had a houseful, but we always had a place to put them. I think I had my bed in every room but the kitchen and bath!

We always had a dog and a cat or two.

—Mom, it wasn't a great house, but you helped make some good memories there!

The ramp that Bill, Gerry and Pastor Charlie built for me.

From the Hicks house we moved to the duplex on Bailey. Mark made some steps for us, and it was a neat little apartment. Amy and the kids would walk over to see us a lot and you would work out in the yard. I loved looking out the door and watching people go by!

After some time we knew we needed more help. Paul and Stacy said they would help us, so we moved to Oklahoma City to live with them.

–Yes, and you were so brave to make that move! It was a BIG step to take, but later, we found out God was watching out for us!!
If we had stayed we would have been injured or killed, because the entire living room ceiling fell in!

It sure was fun watching Willow grow from a baby into a sweet and smart little girl!

–Mom, Oklahoma City was a great place to live! When Paul and Stacy moved to an apartment, we moved to a small apartment as well. It was such a nice place for a short time, but I guess I got a bit nervous being alone again. It's always easier to look back and see how good things are, but God was taking care of us through it all.

Yes, and after a little over a year in OKC, we made the decision to move back with Mark to San Antonio. We stayed seven months with Amy and her family.

So, that brings us to today. We have a really nice house and I am happy here. You and I have a lot of fun playing the marble board, cards and dominoes! I enjoy all the books you get at the library for us to read and talk about!! We go to church and love Pastor Charlie, Cindy and everyone there!! Oh! Charlie, Bill and Gerry came over one Saturday and built a ramp for me! That was so nice of them!!!!!!

–Everyone loves you mom! They always comment on your beautiful smile and happy spirit!

I don't know what is ahead for me, but life is good and we'll make it okay.

More Thoughts and Pictures of Mom's Life...

—Mom always enjoyed traveling and going places with friends and family. This was a very big joy and part of her life! She went many times to visit Linda and Ray, and always had such a good time!!

—You really loved all of Linda's dogs, cat and little puppies! And, her little horse! So cute!

–Even at age 84 and more you loved to travel!

Yes! Going by train was so much fun!! I could get up and walk around and you always packed lunch and dinner. I tried to sleep, but never could! The day went by so quickly!

–We started packing a week ahead and had to plan the food for the day. It was like a mini move!

The first time we went to Oklahoma City was in 2009. Stacy was pregnant with Willow then. Each time was a lot of fun!!

One of the last times I went to Oregon was with Janice.

Linda's house was so beautiful!! I really enjoyed being there with her!!

Oh, and the yard was so beautiful, too! We'd sit out back and visit a long time.

We went out to eat, sight-seeing, too. It was all so pretty there! The flowers were gorgeous!

One of the times I was there, Linda pushed me down the long driveway, so I could see the pond with fish and ducks.

The last time I went alone, was so much fun!! We went to a casino with friends Sandy and Patty, and took a road trip to Sacramento to see Ray and Laura. We went in Linda's motor home, which was so much fun! It was real comfortable, and I really enjoyed that! We spent the night in a mall parking lot, then got up early to pull in at 7:30 just in time for breakfast, We had such a good visit with everyone, and on the way back to Oregon, we had some excitement!

The motor home broke down and we rode in a police car to a truck stop to wait awhile. I said I had to wait 85 years to ride in a police car! (Chuckling to herself)

Every time I went to Linda's was a great fun and I miss going, but it became too hard for me to travel alone.

A Legacy of Love...

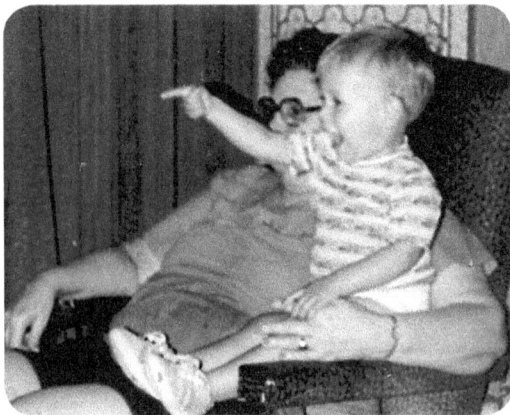

Mom loves her grandchildren and great-grandchildren.

Ray's girls.

Amy's kids.

Paul's girls.

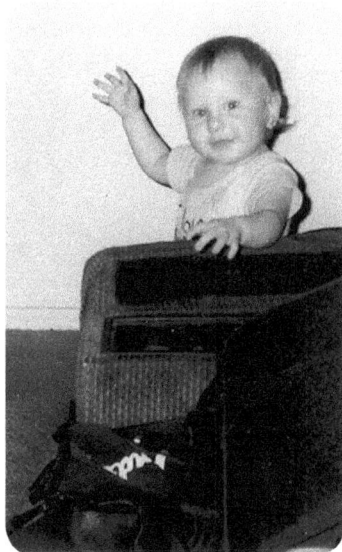
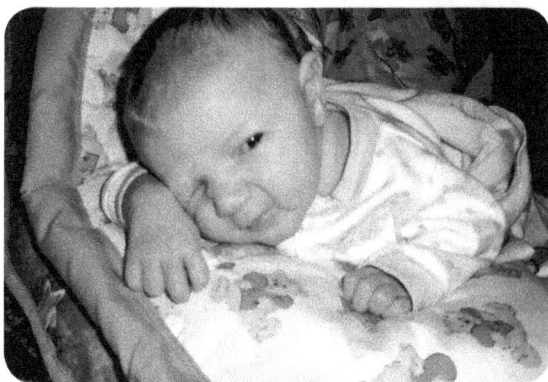

Seven of Beatrice's Great Grandchildren
Caleb, Morgan, Wendy (the Author), Aria, Willow, River, Bella & Noah

Some Final Thoughts....

I have really good memories of my mom through the years.
Maybe some come only from looking at pictures, but I can tell
you as much as I remember, that she loved and took good care of us!
We always had great places to play and neat toys.

And the cute dresses she always had us in! Every Easter we
had a new hat, dress and shoes!!
    I think some of my favorite times were at Easter! She always
made the day so special and full of fun!!

Well, maybe Halloween holds the best memories! She always made sure we had cool costumes to wear.

Christmas was also so great! But, I could go on and on!!

Just making hot cocoa and going to the drive-in was a great time!

Or, going to San Francisco, getting sour dough bread and a hunk of cheese, just to sit by the water and watch boats go by. It didn't matter what the occasion, mom made it special for us!!

That's because mom is a very special lady! And always has been!!

So, this brings us to the present day and it seems right to end the story before her story ends!

She has lived longer than all her brothers and sisters and parents did! She'll probably live to be 100, and I hope she does!!

She'll still be rolling her hair and talking on the phone, but most of all, she'll have her feet up enjoying a good book!

To the end, Bea Duglosch will be a happy woman and will have lived a good life!

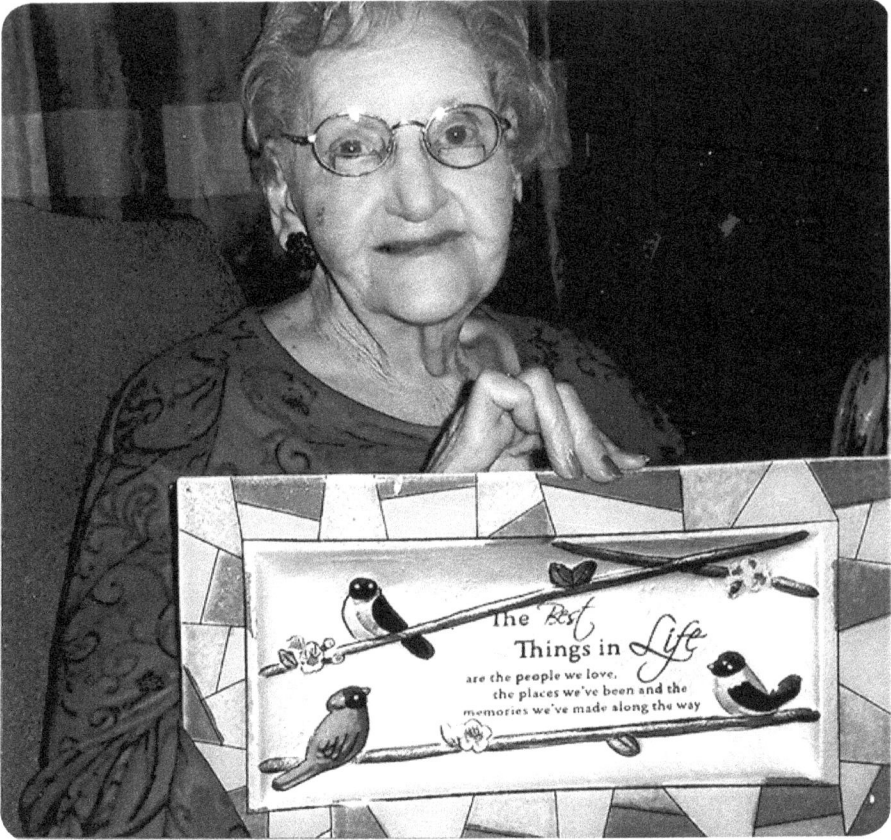

Christmas 2012 was so very special. The entire month was filled with God's blessings!! One of mom gifts was this hand-painted glass picture Amy gave to her. It seems to say just the final thing for this book.

"The Best Things in Life
are the people we love,
the places we've been, and
the memories along the way."

Some Favorite Recipes...

Mom suddenly said how good it would be to share some recipes she made over the years. I thought it was a great idea! Some of our favorite memories are of her cooking for us, so here they are.

Some of Mom's Favorite Recipes

1. Easter Bunny Cake

Make a white 9 x 12 cake. Cool, then cut corners off top to make two triangles. Also, cut about 2" up from bottom and cut that strip in half. Set these pieces aside for the ears and bow tie.

Put cake on a foiled-covered cookie sheet. Cover with icing and coconut. Decorate the face with jelly beans and candy eggs.

Use pipe cleaners for the whiskers.

Color some coconut green and put around the cake and hide candy eggs in it. Enjoy!

Take pictures, as each year it looks a little different!

2. Snowballs-Everyone's favorite Christmas cookie!

2 sticks margarine
2 c. flour
½ c. powdered sugar
1 t. vanilla
½ c. chopped pecans

Mix together and chill for 30 minutes. Make small balls and place on ungreased cookie sheet. Bake at 350° for 10 – 12 minutes. While hot, roll in powdered sugar.

3. Bake and Forget Meringue Cookies
(When I was little, she made these every Christmas)

4 egg whites
1 1/3 c. sugar
2 t. vanilla
semi-sweet choc pieces
½ c. chopped walnuts

Preheat oven to 350°. Cover cookie sheet with foil.

Beat egg whites and gradually add sugar, then vanilla until stiff.
Add chocolate chips and nuts. Fold in. Drop by teaspoon full onto cookie sheet. Can be placed close together. Put pan in oven and turn it off. Leave it in until oven is cool.

4. The Best Thanksgiving Dressing Ever!!

2 bags dressing cubes
8 dried slices of white bread
1 stick of margarine
1 9x12 pan of cornbread (2 Jiffy mixes-prepared)
1 onion, chopped
salt, pepper, poultry seasoning to taste

Mix everything together in a large bowl. Add enough chicken broth to moisten it; add cold water if needed. Dressing should be very moist, but not wet.

Spread mix in 9x13 pan. Bake @ 350° until firm and golden brown, about 1 hour.

5. Chicken Cacciatore

In a big pot, put a cut up chicken with a drizzle of oil. Add salt and pepper to taste.

Layer on top of chicken:
Cut up bell pepper, onion and celery.
Cover with two small cans of tomato sauce; fill one can with water and add that. Make sure all of the chicken and vegetables are covered with liquid.
Cover with lid and let simmer until chicken is done.

Serve over cooked rice.

6. Cake Mix Cookies

   1 box cake mix
   2 eggs
   2 T. flour
   ½ c. packed brown sugar
   ½ c. oil
   ½ c. oatmeal
   ½ c. cereal
   chopped nuts and chocolate chips

   Bake at 350° for 15 minutes or so.

   You can use any mix and whatever makes you happy!

   Our favorite was a yellow mix, maraschino cherries, cut in half, pecans coconut and oatmeal.

7. Mark's favorite Roast

   I always bought a big chuck roast. I'd salt, pepper and garlic salt it and roll it in flour. Then, I'd brown it on both sides.
   Put it in a 9 x 12 pan. Add good sized pieces of carrots, potatoes, and onions, and just a little water.
   Cover with foil and bake at 350° for 2 hours.

   -Her hash made with left over roast was great!!!
   Chop up roast. Cook chopped onion in skillet.
   Add roast and brown gravy.

8. King Ranch Casserole

1 30-count package of corn tortillas
1 can cream of chicken soup
1 can cream of mushroom soup
1 can of milk
1 can Rotel tomatoes
Whole chicken salted, peppered, boiled, and deboned and cubed.

10 oz. Grated cheddar cheese

Mix the soups, milk and tomatoes together. Add cooked and cubed chicken. Stir well and simmer 5-10 minutes.
Layer corn tortillas, soup mixture and cheese in 9 x 12 pan.

Bake at 350° until cheese is melted.

9. My favorite cookies when growing up!

Chocolate Drop Cookies

1 c. firm-packed brown sugar
2/3 c. sugar
1 ¼ c. butter
1 3/4-2 c. flour
2 eggs
2 t. vanilla
¾ c. cocoa
1 t. baking soda
dash salt
1 c. chopped walnuts

Cream butter and both sugar. Add eggs and vanilla and blend well. Combine flour, cocoa, baking soda and salt. Blend into creamed mixture. Stir in nuts. Drop by teaspoon full onto ungreased cookie sheet. Bake at 350° for 8-9 minutes.

Well, I have thought a lot about another favorite recipe and asked Mark. He remembered her pies. I asked Amy, and she said, "Didn't she make some pie a lot when we were kids? I just remember being excited to go visit her, because of SOME-THING she made!"

That about sums it all up! It wasn't so much the pies or cookies or roast, as it was the love she had for us and how it showed best through her cooking.

Afterword
By the Editor

Grandma Bea was a giant in my eyes. My earliest memory of her was when she drove her old blue Datsun down to Weimar, Texas, from San Antonio, for a visit. That morning on the way to school my mother told me that my grandma was coming to see us and would be picking me up from school! The day dragged on for an eternity, but when it was finally over there she was next to her Datsun, beaming with joy. As she always was.

I could recount a hundred memories and more of my grandmother, but I think my mother has done a great job of doing that in this book. I think now is the time to simply finish the story of Beatrice Pearl Dickey.

In 2008 my wife and I moved to Oklahoma. Unbeknownst to me, we moved about fifty miles north of where this book, and my grandmother's life, began. A few years later my mother and grandmother joined my wife and I and our three little daughters, filling out our family and bringing much needed love and warmth.

This book was completed during this period, but sadly it did not get published in time for the star of the story to hold it in her hands. On January 8th of 2015 Grandma Bea passed away peacefully, surrounded by her family.

I was more than Beatrice's grandson; I was her pastor. At the end of her life we were honored to have her as an integral member of our church, and when it came time to honor her memory, I was called upon to take that role. To be able to be the person to stand and speak for my grandmother was the highlight of my life, an honor I doubt will ever be matched.

A Life Well Lived

Beatrice Pearl Dickey lived a life that I think we can all identify with in many ways. She knew hardships and poverty from an early age, growing up in the Great Depression in rural Oklahoma. She knew love in the form of her tightly-knit family, and then love with her first husband, Wendell.

That love did not last and so she knew heartbreak and despair as she was forced to leave her husband and one of her daughters in California and move back home to her family in Texas.

She had deep friendships and spent countless hours cooking, playing games, and enjoying her new life as a single mother. Just as the wounds healed from her failed marriage, she met another man and fell deeply in love. Married for a second time, it seemed that her life was finally complete. Six months later, however, her husband died suddenly from a heart attack, and Bea again knew misery and heartache.

Once again she drew upon the strength found in the arms of her daughter, family and friends, and she overcame. She pulled herself up and began a new job in a new home, deciding that she would not allow the hardships in this life to destroy her.

And in this way, my grandmother, Beatrice Pearl Dickey, forged a legacy that lives on to this day. Through her life, an ordinary life full of love and loss and everything in between, we can see a glimpse of how to live "A Life Well Lived."

Paul Michael Speir
On Beatrice Pearl Dickey's 94th birthday,
November, 13th, 2019

A loving mother and daughter,
Wendolyn & Beatrice